Speak, Cairn

poems by

Lisa Kundrat

Finishing Line Press
Georgetown, Kentucky

Speak, Cairn

For my parents, Frank and Laurie Kundrat

Copyright © 2018 by Lisa Kundrat
ISBN 978-1-63534-439-4 First Edition
All rights reserved under International and Pan-American Copyright Conventions.
No part of this book may be reproduced in any manner whatsoever without written permission from the publisher, except in the case of brief quotations embodied in critical articles and reviews.

ACKNOWLEDGMENTS & NOTES

"Always return with an extra tree for Soyla Luz" was first published by *Verse Wisconsin*.

The form of "Hobo's Song" was inspired by "String of Pearls," song lyrics by Laurelyn Dossett.

Thank you to the Terry Family Foundation in Madison, Wisconsin and the Anderson Center at Tower View in Red Wing, Minnesota for the inspiring and quiet work spaces.

Thank you to all my teachers.

Publisher: Leah Maines
Editor: Christen Kincaid
Cover Art: Boulder Fields, by Elizabeth Claire Rose,
    https://elizabethclairerose.com/
Author Photo: Kristy Kundrat
Cover Design: Elizabeth Maines McCleavy

Printed in the USA on acid-free paper.
Order online: www.finishinglinepress.com
    also available on amazon.com

Author inquiries and mail orders:
Finishing Line Press
P. O. Box 1626
Georgetown, Kentucky 40324
U. S. A.

Table of Contents

Cairn 1

Boreal
You will come to a town where only children will
    speak to you 4
This place of water is full of drowning 5
The hunter's shack will be empty 6
Balance yourself with your hands on the gunwales 7
The northern lights are only seen in winter
    when it's always dark 8
Your guidebook leads to someone's bedroom,
    someone's grave 9

Hot Springs, Montana
Man with a Limp Who Runs the Cottages 12
Leroy, Who Runs the Pools Tourists Don't
Know About 13
Man with Chronic Pain 14
Natural Hot Springs Connoisseur 15
Woman Standing Outside the Laundromat 16
Rancher with a Pleasant Disposition 17

The Eco-City
Plantings in the Eco-City 20
Learning a Language 21
The Balcony 22
Mercedes 23
Always return with an extra tree for Soyla Luz 25

Hobo's Song 27

Think of the long trip home.
Should we have stayed at home and thought of here?
Where should we be today?
 —Elizabeth Bishop, "Questions of Travel"

I am an orphan on God's highway,
but I'll share my troubles if you go my way.
 —Gillian Welch, "Orphan Girl"

Speak, Cairn takes the reader on a trip through a variety of natural landscapes (boreal forest by canoe, fruit-tree planting in an equatorial eco-city, soaking in mineral baths in Montana). The reader connects with people along the way who are rooted in the place the reader travels through. The reader continues to move, feeling moments of connection, but mostly alien and lost. The collection is book-ended by two poems concerning cairns, markers on a trail that show people where to go. As alone as we may feel as we travel through the world looking for home, when we add a stone to a cairn, we are connected to our fellow travelers. "We speak to each other through stones." The final poem, "Hobo's Song," says, "We kneel before the world's brokenness,/a puzzle that will never be finished./We build to repair, to make whole,/to connect the pieces, stone by stone." As much as our human world is broken and each traveler alone, these poems reconnect us to each other and to the earth, like a human-made stack of stones.

Cairn

We speak to each other through stones.
We kneel before the cairn like prayer.
The hard stones comfort those who roam:
you're not lost, you are here, where we were.

We kneel before the cairn like prayer.
We wander, searching for the next message:
you're not lost, you are here, where we were.
To belong we surrender our wildness.

The landscape is filled with messages,
stacked stones that comfort those who roam.
To belong we surrender our wildness,
we speak to each other through stones.

Boreal

You will come to a town where only children will speak to you.

A boy with a snot- and dirt-covered face asks you
to watch him run and jump from the docks. The dogs
follow you everywhere. Because you are lucky, the pilot
outside his floatplane will also speak to you, of the boy
who was stupid and lost himself while hunting
in the Bush, of the place where you can break through
to find the next river. True your canoe to the line he made
with his arm, cross over to the far side of the water,
and find the gap in the trees, the place where you
will enter a bog, will carry your boat through the marsh,
will resist the mudded water sucking you up to your waist.

This place of water is full of drowning.

On one stretch of land stands a man who tells you his wife
has been carried away by helicopter. Wasn't room enough
for his weight. He must wait for their return. They had been spilled
into the river. He had floated to shore with his paddle and camera.
His wife's jacket, her hair, her body had been caught by a tree
lying half in the water, the branches holding her. He had no way
of crossing. They had forgotten their knapsack where the ground trail
met the river. Inside was a second jacket, inside this was a map,
a half-eaten apple, a sea scallop in the chalk hold of limestone.

The hunter's shack will be empty.

Every piece of land in this place of water has socks scattered
here and there. As if someone took them off before sleep, will
return later to sleep again. Pull your canoe over and walk up the shore.
A structure built hastily on chopped away weeds, over bent and torn
saplings. The door hangs open. Inside, more socks. A stove
filled with ashes. Moldy, wet floorboards, the ones in the corner
specked with fish hooks and black. Outside, silence, an empty yard.
As if someone had just built it, as if no one had been here for years,
as if someone had just left, as if no one would ever return,
as if someone will return at any moment, as if someone is already here.

Balance yourself with your hands on the gunwales.

One leg centered on the boat's bottom, use the other to push off from sand. A scraping. But the river will take you. The yellow head of a wolf pokes out from reeds looking for the source of this noise. Finds you with its eyes, disappears. A small black bear watching you from shore will only begin to cry out as you pass. The skulls of sturgeon, the size of small children's line the shore. Above them, nets hang from branches, long dried.

The northern lights are only seen in winter when it's always dark.

Standing on a tower made of driftwood, watch the white dot
of a polar bear moving across the tundra's flat green. The policeman
puts hand to holstered gun. He offered you a ride in the cab of his truck.
You sat behind the bars in back reading the graffiti etched by the teens'
fingernails in metal. *Finally some normals,* he said as he drove
down the gravel embankment along the purple brown water of the bay.
The lights show north across the tundra. But the wind—
he says, squinting to remember that cold blowing off the bay.

Your guidebook leads to someone's bedroom, someone's grave.

You find your own way, you don't know where
you've been. Again you pull to the side. You stand
on slabs of limestone. Terns swoop over the green
crumbling bluffs. You drop to the ground. Swirls
of coral rise up from within the rock. A finger
touched to tongue, touched to stone, causes a sea star
the size of a minnow's eye to lift dark beige against white.
You are squatting on what used to be the bottom of the ocean.
The cold wind tastes of salt. Ahead, after thirty wind-blown
silent miles, lies a town filled with shacks, an opening filled with ice.

Hot Springs, Montana

Man with a Limp Who Runs the Cottages

Furnished rooms, equipped kitchenettes, hot mineral water runs right into the private bathrooms. Use the dishes from the office kitchen, but remember to bring them back so we can make dinner. If I could walk farther, I'd walk out of this town and all the way to Lydia's house on the edge of the Buffalo Preserve. We'd walk all over the hills, buffalo like fallen boulders lumbering in the dark. We'd be close enough to smell the musky hides, buffalo fur caught in low-lying branches would fall off and collect in our hair, on our clothes. We'd walk all night before I'd walk back here.

Leroy, Who Runs the Pools Tourists Don't Know About

Watch out honey you just about saw the dark side of the moon. Let me get into this pool. The schoolteacher types always come for the mud baths. Leroy this, Leroy that, having the time of their lives. Always wanting my certificates: certified mud bunny. The girls from Missoula are the biggest hoot. Bringing their crystals on the night of the full moon, laying them along the edge of the pool. The people called this place Big Medicine when they first found it. Even better with my cigarettes right here, under the grate of the filter.

Man with Chronic Pain

Walking back to my room after the soak, I feel every inch of my skin forthright, the usual dull ache of nerve endings pulled taut. October and already snow crunches under the boots. The doctor said these hot mineral pools springing from beneath the ground would ease the pain I'm used to feeling, but not used to. My daughter lost to me. I left what was left of everything, which was nothing. To come to this half-rundown place. This place half closer to how it originally sprang.

Natural Hot Springs Connoisseur

I wouldn't say the water over there at Leroy's place is *dirty* water, but *heavy* water. It's heavier than this water. It holds you down, leaches what it wants from you, fills you with itself. Replaces some of your weight with its own. Believe me, when I saw you on the street today I didn't say hello not because I didn't want to acknowledge your presence, but because I didn't hear you call out my name.

Woman Standing Outside the Laundromat

This place rundown due to meth. Which is to say the devil. I know because I've seen. This place full of good people under the influence. Which is to say people who may be lost. The other day one comes up when I'm inside my RV and steals my axe off the bumper. Just takes it. I'm here with the husband. Getting some soaks in. Been coming here some thirty years. Which is to say longer than you can remember. These pools keep something here bigger than the devil, but he's getting bigger all the time.

Rancher with a Pleasant Disposition

Man, I love this place. Good soaking. About the only thing that helps my hip—the old injury plaguing daylong stock rides. Makes me think I might need to find something new to do. I don't know what. That was my girlfriend who left the pool. Says call them horses not stock. Says how can you have no ideas for what to do. But she doesn't know what it is to have no idea who you are. Sits in this hot pool and remains only what she is—a stone stewing in this shifting combination of silt and salts. But me I am the salts.

The Eco-City

Plantings in the Eco-City

You've arrived during the rainy season
to a soaked bamboo awning, to soaked seedlings
lining a crumbling brick wall. The kids lift
these small trees into the wheelbarrow, name each
as they set it down: *hierba luisa, papaya, limón.*
How could you know of what can and cannot
be planted? The eco-club kids' white canvas
shoes somehow spotless. The feet gingerly move
between mud ruts. Your hands, your rubber boots
caked with muck. But what of Mercedes' hands,
of her bare feet, which jump between the green
beaded pools filled with swimming tadpoles?

Learning a Language

Your tree-planting partner, Marcelo, asks you a question and follows with *sí-o-no-sí-o-no-sí-o-no* so fast, you're confused, say no, uh sí? Next thing you know you're in the back of a pickup driving into the countryside. When you stop, a farmer hands you a garbage bag bulging with passion fruit. Marcelo nods at you, satisfied. When you first stepped off the bus into this town next to the ocean, people said words to you, but the words were just sounds. Now, the sounds start to correspond to pictures in your mind. You begin to see that as long as two people decide they are going to understand each other, you can communicate with drawings in the mud. The farmer takes you to his field, pulls up a plant from the soil, points to the white peanut-shaped foam on the roots, says, *maní*. You smile—you never knew that's how peanuts grew.

The Balcony

Only fire ants flood into your bathroom. No water
has run for days, no click clack signaling water
flowing through pipes and you'd rush to fill
as many pots as possible to clean the counters, floors,
your body, before it turns off again. Your rain bucket
has been low for days, smells of algae. You're standing
on the balcony watching the clouds gather over the ocean,
a bolt of lightning hits the surface, thunder cracks
open the sky and you fall to your knees. Go inside
take off your clothes, cover yourself with soap, run out
onto the bricks, naked in the darkness, water and soap
streaming off your skin. You are dancing yourself clean.

Mercedes

You next see her when you turn,
she's calling your name, pushing her way
through a crowd in the bus station—

living there now. Mercedes, who perched
atop the compost pile in the wheelbarrow,
singing to the people walking home.

Now she humors you with a smile
when you ask what she wants
to be. She's nine, and takes your hand,

leads you to the right bus, rides
with you to the airport. You're a child
who's found a child. Both far from home.

You buy her ice cream, give her money,
tell her it'd be best to go home, too.
But you both know—

You'll remember her bare feet
running across the pavement
until she disappears into darkness.

You'll remember she was alone,
you left. You'd be wrong to forget
her spunk, joy, courage, grit.

When a woman's fingers grip
your arm, her baby's mouth open
and covered in dirt, you look away.

But Mercedes turns to her, looks
her in the eyes, puts all the money
you just gave Mercedes into her hand.

Always return with an extra tree for Soyla Luz

whose parents named her *I am the light*,
who'll shrug and smile if you ask about it,
and who'll move to her garden to tuck this
coveted limón into the algae-covered soil
in a corner, behind banana leaves, enough
sunlight coming through holes in the fence,
the tree hidden enough from dogs and kids.
Upstairs, her grandkids hoot and tackle
each other like the wrestlers on TV,
take turns being thrown over your shoulder
and spun. Soyla laughs and stirs soup
on the stove. What made you think
your company was enough? They hand you
a globe and you show them from where
on the map you came and they all point
there, too, to say that's where they will go.

Hobo's Song
After "String of Pearls," by Laurelyn Dossett

Holding a stone is holding a hand,
human presence stacked up, balanced,
the smooth weight pulls me toward home—
I'm no longer alone when I add a stone.

An exile from paradise, a flightless bird,
I wander for miles without speaking words.
Rocks are words, stacked up like a poem—
to join a conversation is to add a stone.

Saying their names I add to the rows,
each rock is another person I've known.
This cairn can't lead me back home,
but I'm there again when I add a stone.

We kneel before the world's brokenness,
a puzzle that will never be finished.
We build to repair, to make whole,
to connect the pieces, stone by stone.

Lisa Kundrat's sense of adventure and love of teaching have led her many places. She has canoed 500 miles through Ontario to Hudson Bay, directed a fruit tree-planting project on the coast of Ecuador, and won a golden cowbell at a cross-country ski race in Wisconsin. She has guided wilderness trips in Montana, taught writing at the University of Wisconsin, and worked with youth to create community festivals in Minnesota.

Her poems and writing have won awards, been published in periodicals, and been made into songs and performed in an opera.

Kundrat grew up in Saint Cloud, Minnesota and has a BA from the University of Montana-Missoula and a MFA in poetry from the University of Wisconsin-Madison. She lives in Montana with her husband, Andy.

Learn more or contact her through her website: lisakundrat.com

www.ingramcontent.com/pod-product-compliance
Lightning Source LLC
LaVergne TN
LVHW041508070426
835507LV00012B/1424